IMAGES OF ENGLAND

KNARESBOROUGH

IMAGES OF ENGLAND

KNARESBOROUGH

ARNOLD KELLETT

TEMPUS

Dedicated to all the older Crag Rats (people privileged to have been born and bred in Knaresborough), especially those who have shared with me their photographs and memories.

Frontispiece: A tranquil scene from the 1930s showing Knaresborough in its beautiful setting on the Nidd.

First published 1995
New edition 2003

Tempus Publishing Limited
The Mill, Brimscombe Port,
Stroud, Gloucestershire, GL5 2QG

British Library Cataloguing in Publication Data.
A catalogue record for this book is available from the British Library.

ISBN 0 7524 3017 3
Typesetting and origination by Tempus Publishing Limited
Printed in Great Britain by Midway Colour Print, Wiltshire

Contents

The Knaresborough seal carved in stone on the old Council Offices, showing the barbican gate of the Castle and an oak leaf representing the ancient Forest of Knaresborough.

Many of these photographs are from the horse and cart days – but modern times lie ahead: Taylor and Sons, game and poultry dealers of Kirkgate, already have on their cart a brand–new telephone number – 17X!

Introduction

When I accepted the invitation from the publishers to compile this book I knew it was not going to be easy. The fact is that, picturesque and historic though Knaresborough certainly is, it does not have an existing archive of old photographs. It is true that, over the years, various postcards have appeared, and there are several collections of these, including my own publication *Knaresborough in Old Picture Postcards* (1984). However, although I have included some postcards, this new book is far more wide-ranging, with photographs begged and borrowed from all over the place. Many of these have never been published in any form, and some have not seen the light of day for decades. For this reason alone I must emphasise that *everything in this book is copyright* – not to be reproduced without permission.

It would, of course, have been far easier to edit some existing collection, but this would not have given me the stimulating experience of rooting around, doing interesting detective work and, above all, listening to the vivid reminiscences of Knaresborough people who have been kind enough to allow me to use their old photos. I really have appreciated the willingness with which family albums have been plundered, pictures taken from their frames, and drawers, cupboards and memories ransacked. I have ended up with far more photographs than there was space for, resulting in agonising choices and complex balancing-acts, but I trust that the final selection of at least 250 will be sufficiently representative to give a real insight into the most recent phase of Knaresborough's long and lively history. Readers who wish to learn about the earlier phases should consult, for example, my / (1991), where further illustrations can also be seen.

To set these photographs in their historical context we must realise that they represent the mere tip of an iceberg which goes down deep into the ocean of time. Long before photography became established Knaresborough had a succession of fascinating historical events of which we have little pictorial record. If only some local photographer had been able to capture, for example, the Angles building their first settlement of Knarresburg, or the Normans building the first stone castle, or King John hunting in the Forest of Knaresborough . . . In 1985 I turned up the fact (then unknown even to the Royal Almonry) that in 1210 the same King John fed and clothed thirteen paupers in our town – the first known record of a Royal Maundy. If only we had a photograph of that memorable occasion! Or photos of other royal visitors, such as Edward III and Queen Philippa, or Richard II, here as a prisoner. Then, perhaps, a few pictures of action during the siege of Knaresborough Castle at the close of l644 . . .

The Civil War is a good point from which to start setting the scene for our photographs. After the fall of the Castle the economy of Knaresborough diversified.

What had since Norman times been essentially a garrison town now became the first place in England to have its name linked with the mineral springs of Spa in Belgium. Using the town as a base, health-seekers came here to visit the 'Spaws of Knaresborough' and to 'take the waters' at what soon developed into the substantial town of Harrogate. Even after Harrogate became established as a premier Spa, visitors still came to Knaresborough – this time travelling in the reverse direction, with a therapeutic stroll around our attractive scenery as part of 'the cure'.

So when the earliest of these photographs were taken Knaresborough was already a well-known tourist spot. Tourism, however, was by no means the mainstay of Knaresborough's economy – a situation which remains true today. Reflected in the earlier photographs are local industries such as the manufacture of linen (good enough to supply all the royal household), the related trade of ropemaking, the production of leather and the allied trade of the cordwainer or shoemaker. Then, of course, the market, dating from at least the twelfth century, has always been of great importance, serving as an outlet for farmers from miles around, with an additional market for livestock which, as these photos show, ensured that the High Street was well manured. Until 1974, when we became part of the Harrogate District, Knaresborough was self-governing, for centuries electing two M.P.s, later being administered by the Improvement Commissioners, who were replaced in 1894 by the elected Knaresborough Urban District Council.

Alongside the trades, crafts and services providing employment there has always been a very active social life here. Sightseers who come to Knaresborough may not realise that it has such a strong sense of community, with a great variety of organisations and activities which have nothing to do with tourism – churches, schools, charities, societies, sports clubs, special events and celebrations of all kinds. It is this that I have come across more than anything else in assembling these local photographs. This book is, in fact, far more about people than places. People are the very stuff of history. (But why, oh why, do we so rarely identify them by writing names and dates on the backs of photos?!)

As in the case of my four earlier books on Knaresborough I cannot claim to have covered everything in this new volume. The survival of photographs is largely a matter of chance, and I have found lots of gaps with no picture to fill them. It is not even the survival of the fittest. Some of the very best photographs will have been lost for ever, and the saddest part of preparing a book like this is to hear, again and again, of old plates and prints that have simply been thrown away.

How true it is that one picture is worth a thousand words! Even so, I hope readers will also enjoy the historical commentary in the captions, in which I have included as much relevant detail as I have been able to unearth. Pictures and words together should then help us to contemplate something of Knaresborough's recent past. From a population of around 5,000, when the oldest photos were taken, the town has almost trebled in size – growing far too big, far too fast, in my opinion. Yet there is still a real affection for what remains of old Knaresborough, and there can be no doubt that its friendly yet independent spirit lives on . . . Let us, then, take both interest and pride in the generations that have gone before us and live in such a way that we, in our turn, will be worthy of being recorded by the cameras that cannot lie.

Arnold Kellett

one

Old-World
Knaresborough

Above: Unspoilt Waterside as it looked after 1872, when the roof of the Parish Church was restored to its original height. The old Almshouses (left foreground) were demolished when the Claro Laundry was built here in 1902.

Left: The ruined keep of Knaresborough Castle towering above the tranquil River Nidd, some 120 feet below. When this scene was photographed in about 1880 the Castle grounds had not been landscaped, nor had Waterside been fully developed. There were, however, a number of houses, the linen mill, and the building in the foreground, once the indigo mill, where dried plants were ground to supply deep blue for the adjacent dyehouse.

This remarkably early photograph of Knaresborough (taken no later than 1865) shows the original Knaresborough Workhouse – the large building in front of the Parish Church. The Workhouse, built in 1737, accommodated about 40 paupers, looked after by a Master who was paid £26.15s. a year. In 1793 he complained in his report 'As one goes out another comes in. Gentlemen, I think they come from all parts of the world to Knaresborough, for they know where they get much made on. Pox take 'em all!'

Typical old cottages with their pantile roofs, formerly in Castle Yard. If only property like this had been well maintained and restored Knaresborough would have been even more attractive. Unfortunately so many similar dwellings were demolished by the Knaresborough Urban District Council in a slum clearance programme of houses 'totally unfit for habitation'.

Knaresborough Castle, rebuilt in 1312 by Edward II, once had twelve towers as well as the great keep. Taken by the Parliamentarians in December, 1644, it was officially dismantled as a former Royalist stronghold in 1648. However, like the defiant stump of an old tooth, part of the sturdy keep survives, and commands a glorious view over the Nidd gorge. This photo dates from around 1905.

The dungeon of Knaresborough Castle as it has looked ever since 1312. The beauty of the twelve graceful arches supported by the central pillar would not have been appreciated by the prisoners, manacled to the wall. With walls fifteen feet thick and only one tiny window the dungeon made a perfect 'cooler', and was also used for storage.

The Old Manor House is one of the most venerable dwellings in Knaresborough, dating from medieval times. This chequered appearance, which seems to have influenced other buildings in the town, dates from before the late nineteenth century restoration made by R.F. Roundell, M.P. for Skipton, whose family had lived in Knaresborough since the fifteenth century.

The Old Manor House was for many years a popular café with a pleasant riverside garden. Inside could be seen the roof-tree, fine oak panelling and the bed in which Cromwell slept, probably moved here from Cromwell House in High Street, where he once stayed.

Left: A 1930s view looking down Water Bag Bank, so called because part of the town's water supply came from the river below and was carried up here in leather bags on the backs of donkeys and horses, as well as in pails carried by women at a halfpenny a time.

Below: Age-old Manor Cottage, at the bottom of Water Bag Bank, is the only surviving thatched building in Knaresborough, but thatchers like these must have been kept busy in the old days, as early prints and documents show that this was a common form of roofing.

Beech Hill, off Kirkgate, a typical Knaresborough street scene in the 1920s before the old cottages, with shuttered windows and crumbling plaster, were pulled down and replaced – rather than restored. The Manor of Beech Hill, one of the most ancient parts of the town, was originally a small estate surrounding the Parish Church. It was actually a prebend created in 1230 by the Archbishop of York, bringing in revenue to the prebendary. It was a self-governing area, with courts and constables of its own. In this photo we see Teddy Carass talking to his sister Peggy, who is holding a puppy. Another little girl looks on, and another dog, basking on the sunlit cobbles, seems to guard the boy reading a book.

Paradise Row, Fisher Gardens, in the late 1920s, shortly before demolition. Note the wooden hatchways of the coal-cellars. Opposite stood a row of outside toilets or privies. The houses look substantial enough, deserving modernisation rather than destruction. Is that what the housewife seen here was thinking?

Houses ready for demolition at the bottom of Fisher Gardens. Handsomely faced with local magnesian limestone these were too lightly written off as slums, and would surely have been saved by modern conservationists. Fisher Gardens, I assume, were named after the Knaresborough gardener, William Fisher (d. 1743), who laid out Studley Park.

Abbey Road as it looked towards the end of the nineteenth century. To the left is the entrance to the quarry, marked by a fine gas lamp, symbolic of the fact that Knaresborough had its own gas supply at a very early date, the first street lamps being lit on 23 September, 1824.

Conyngham Hall, Knaresborough.

In contrast to the humble dwellings seen above we have one of Knaresborough's stately homes. Conyngham Hall was built on the Tudor site of Coghill Hall towards the end of the eighteenth century by John Carr. The name dates from 1796, when it was sold to the Countess of Conyngham. In 1856 it became the home of Basil Woodd, first Chairman of the Council. From 1905 it was owned by the Charlesworth family, who from 1934 to 1942 leased it to Sir Harold Mackintosh.

Above: An early 1900s view of the beginning of Abbey Road from across the river. Dominating the huddle of cottages is the House in the Rock, with its mock battlements picked out in white. On the riverbank can be seen the rug factory, with skins and fleeces stretched out to dry.

Left: A photograph of the portrait shown to visitors to the House in the Rock. This is of 'Sir' Thomas Hill, a poor linen-weaver, who with the help of his son, dug into the crag and built a remarkable home there between 1770 and 1791. He called it Fort Montague in honour of his benefactress the Duchess of Buccleugh, flew a Union Jack and fired a two-pounder cannon from the battlements, and printed his own bank notes.

Right: Near the House in the Rock is the much older Chapel of Our Lady of the Crag, carved out of the rock by John the Mason in 1408 as a thank-offering for his child's life, saved from a rockfall. The entrance to the tiny shrine is guarded by a soldier, possibly one of the Knights Templar, whose face had been worn away, but replaced in concrete. The Edwardian lady, seen in 1907, is Mary Ann Hill.

Left: Mrs Ann Hill, mother of the lady above, at the upper entrance to the House in the Rock, with her parrot, 'Slingsby', named after the family that owned this and so many other parts of Knaresborough. She was widowed at the age of 54, when her husband, greatgrandson of the original builder, 'Sir' Thomas Hill, fell down the stone stairway inside and broke his neck.

Knaresborough High Street in the early 1900s, complete with cattle, not being driven through, but there as part of the livestock market, which was not moved to a purpose-built site until 1907. The mooing and manuring contrasted strangely with the dignified façade of arched windows of the Knaresborough and Claro Bank, built in 1858.

Another view of the High Street cattle-market, looking up the hill to the Crown Hotel. On the right is Bradley's sweetshop, a receiving office for the Jubilee Steam Laundry. Watched by the cattle appear to be a clergyman pushing his bike and a policeman standing under the lamp post.

Looking down the Edwardian High Street. Behind the carriage is Abbot's the fruiterers, to the right of which is Southwell's the chemists and Bowler's the outfitters. The great beech tree is in front of Beech House, home of Dr. W.J. Forbes.

The upper part of High Street showing, on the right, the entrance to Park Square, with a notice indicating that here was the exchange of the National Telephone Service. This was formerly called White Horse Yard, and the large gabled building was originally an inn named after Eugene Aram, whose little school was in the yard.

A late-Victorian view of Knaresborough Market, one of many local photographs taken by G.E. Arnold, a versatile man who was best known as organist of St. John's Parish Church. The market has been held every Wednesday since at least 1310, when this day was confirmed as market day by the Charter of Edward II. In earlier centuries Knaresborough was noted for locally-grown liquorice, then cherries, and by the end of the eighteenth century this was one of the biggest corn markets in Yorkshire. The gas lamp seen here is a real curiosity, because earlier in the century it had replaced the badly-eroded Market Cross – a Victorian lamp post stuck on the circular base built in 1709!

Opposite: Though remarkably picturesque, Knaresborough knew poverty and hardship, as is illustrated by this scene on the steps of the Market Cross. Taken by C. A. Brotherton, it was exhibited in 1939 with the title 'Down and Out'. This is an eloquent testimony to what many experienced during the period of depression which preceded the Second World War. We can just see, to the left of this dejected tramp, a sign of modern times – the base of the electric lamp, which by the 1930s had replaced the old gas lamp. A new Market Cross was finally provided in 1953 by Cecil Naden, the monumental mason, who tried to give it an air of antiquity by carving this date on it in Roman numerals.

The classic view of Knaresborough that has remained virtually unchanged since 1851, the year the railway viaduct was rebuilt following its collapse, when almost completed, in 1848. Though the architectural authority Niklaus Pevsner described the way in which the line had been allowed to cut across the gorge as 'one of the most notable railway crimes of England', we tend to agree with J.B. Priestley that the viaduct 'adds a double beauty to the scene' when it is reflected in the river, as in this view by A.E. Jones, one of thousands painted and photographed over the years. I like to think that though the Castle was destroyed on the orders of Cromwell he was unable to touch this magnificent view from it. Unique in the British Isles, it is Knaresborough's greatest asset – and nothing must be allowed to spoil it.

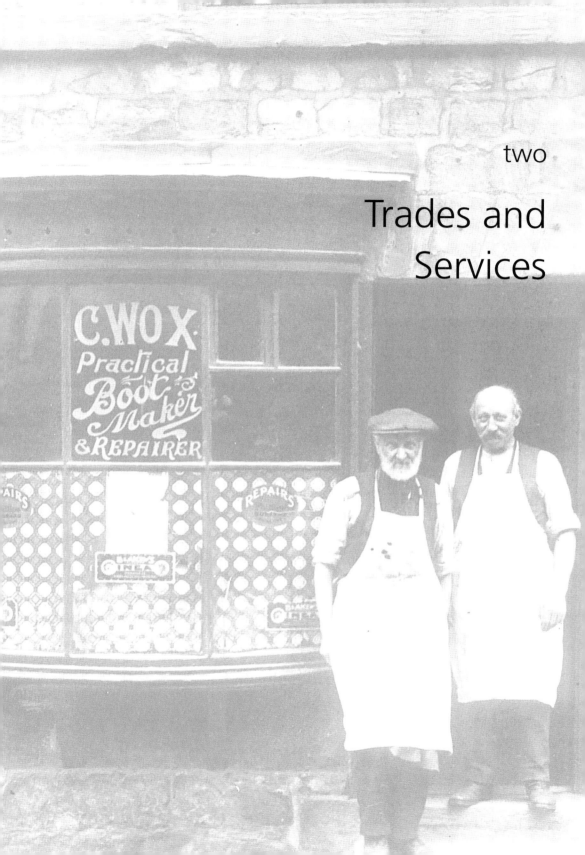

two

Trades and Services

Workers at Walton's linen mill in 1900. The production of linen had been a cottage industry in Knaresborough since Tudor times, but from 1811 was concentrated in the riverside Castle Mill, built in 1791. The workforce had reached 423 by 1851, the year George Hemshall received the Prince Albert Medal for weaving a seamless linen shirt. His son, John Hemshall, the firm's accountant, is the man in the top hat on the back row. By this time Walton's employed only around 100, but it still had the distinction of supplying linen to Queen Victoria's household.

The weft-winding department of Walton's Castle Mill in 1935. By this stage the flax had been retted, boiled, bleached, heckled, dressed, dyed and spun, and was now ready for weaving. Life in the linen trade was hard, the workers starting their day here at 6 am., and sometimes working until 6 pm.

Above: Weaving linen at Walton's on a Hattersley loom. Woven into the tea-towels, for example, were names such as Balmoral, Sandringham and Buckingham Palace, and the firm was able to advertise its 'Knaresborough Linens, now used in all the royal palaces', the quality being world-famous.

Right: Miss Harriet Wilson, retiring in 1935 at the age of 75, after working as a weft-winder at Walton's for 62 years. Long and loyal service was typical of Knaresborough. Harriet's father and grandfather each worked at Walton's for 48 years, her sister for 33 and her brother for 23.

Above: Here we see Harriet Wilson with some of her fellow workers outside the linen mill, being given a final handshake – presumably by the managing director, Joseph Carson, who died that same year (1935) aged 51. Founded in 1785 by Christopher Walton, the firm ceased manufacturing linen in 1972, and in 1984 Castle Mill was sold by Harrogate Borough Council for private residential development.

Left: A rare Victorian photograph of the old ropeworks on Crag Top, showing (from left) Thomas Owram Johnson, Edwin James Johnson and George Johnson. The Johnsons had a shop in High Street which sold 'ropes, cords, twines, halters, reins, ploughlines, clotheslines etc.' Twine was made at Bridge Mill, near Low Bridge, but this Crag Top 'ropewalk' (a length of ground for twisting and tarring rope) was typical of the scores of small family firms all over Knaresborough.

Cordwainers, or shoemakers, have for centuries been an important trade in Knaresborough, and were once so numerous that the town kept the feast of St. Crispin (25 October), patron saint of cobblers. Here we see Charles Wox (right), 'practical bootmaker and repairer', outside his High Street shop, with Mr. Bateson, in about 1900.

William ('Billie') Wox at work. He carried on his father's trade of shoemaking and repairing in the same shop, 72 High Street, till his death in 1978. This is still one of the most attractive buildings in High Street, dating from at least 1611.

DESTRUCTION BY FIRE OF KNARESBRO LEATHER WORKS JAN 28.08.

Knaresborough Fire Brigade in the late 1890s, one of the earliest photos of the volunteers prepared to devote themselves to dealing with fires and other emergencies in the town – a tradition that is still with us. By this time the Fire Brigade was under the auspices of the Knaresborough Urban District Council, which explains the presence of the man in the bowler hat, George Wilson, the surveyor and captain. These dependable-looking men, mostly from appropriate trades – blacksmiths, plumbers, slaters and joiners – gave their services free until 1920, when they received an official £2 per annum. The man with the splendid beard in the centre is T. Lund, the waterman. The sergeant (back row) is Abel Mason. The fire engine was kept in Drill Yard, Chapel Street, and the keys were kept at the sergeant's house. The firemen were summoned by the bell in the Town Hall and one behind the Commercial, now the Borough Bailiff.

Opposite above: Low Bridge, formerly called March Bridge (from an old word for a boundary) and earlier still the site of a ford, the main route into Knaresborough. To the left we see the Mother Shipton, known in Victorian times as the Dropping Well inn, on the right March House (1745), the name Bridge House being comparatively recent. On the riverbank skins and fleeces are stretched out to dry for Holgate's rug factory.

Opposite below: Sellar's leatherworks, at the junction of Brewerton Street with Union Street, after its complete destruction by fire on Saturday afternoon 28 January, 1908. Though the Knaresborough fire engine was supplemented by two from Harrogate the building was reduced to a shell.

Knaresborough Fire Brigade in 1947, the first time it ossessed an up-to-date Leyland fire engine, bought by the Council. Front: A. Bailey (Harrogate), Bob Whitehouse (Station Officer). Second row, from left: G. Grocott, W. Malthouse, H. Newbould, A. Mather, F. Wiseman, K. Craven, Back: B. Rumfitt, B. Whincup, J. Maskill, J. Hamley, D. Halliday, C. Capin, H. Clegg, Joe Jordan (Sub Officer). Continuity of service is illustrated by the fact that there were two other Malthouses in the Brigade in the early 1900s.

Knaresborough Fire Brigade in 1956, on the completion of the new fire station in Gracious Street. Sitting, from left: B. Whincup, S. Cleasby, J. Maskill, Bob Whitehouse (Station Officer), Joe Jordan (Sub Officer), G. Hill, C. Hill. Standing: J. Hamley, G. Simpson, A. Mather, H. Coe, D. Watson, R. Dobby, M. Plewes, C. Capin, B. Jordan, W. Malthouse, B. Nicholson.

The earliest known photograph of a Knaresborough physician. This was Dr. Peter Murray, who came here in 1803 and set up the Dispensary for Free Medicine, originally at the top of Castle Ings, later rebuilt in Castle Yard in 1853. Described as 'a constant friend of the poor', in 1826 he retired because of his own ill health to Scarborough, where this photograph was presumably taken in his later years.

An early glimpse of Knaresborough Hospital, built as a workhouse in Stockwell Road in 1858. Designed in mock Tudor style by Isaac Shutt (architect of Harrogate's Royal Pump Room) it consisted of a male and female hospital, a matron's and children's block, administrative block etc. Housing up to around 300 inmates, it was known locally as 'the Grubber' even after its adaptation as a modern geriatric hospital.

Knaresborough Post Office workers in the early 1900s. On the right, holding the bicycle, is John Patrick, wearing his medals from the Boer War. He gave a total of thirty years' service as a postman. In 1906 the Post Office in High Street was open from 7 am to 8 pm. There were three deliveries a day, and five collections from the main pillar boxes, with one at 5.50 pm on Sundays. There were sub-offices in Briggate and at Scriven.

The World's End inn near High Bridge, as it looked before it was replaced by the present building in 1898. The licensee was Charles Blenkhorn, whose notice on the gable end offers not only 'Good Stabling' but also 'Pleasure boats for hire'. In addition Charles Blenkhorn served as postmaster, and in the early 1900s his sister, Miss C. Blenkhorn, was postmistress.

Right: Sturdy's boatlanding, at the foot of the Castle steps. Founded by Richard Sturdy (1837-1913) around the middle of the nineteenth century, this complemented the later firm of Blenkhorn's near High Bridge, and was licensed for 140 boats as against Blenkhorn's 90. The wooden hut like a sentry box was used for storing oars. This photo dates from about 1902. Ten years later young George Smith started work here, rowing the Penny Ferry across to the Dropping Well estate.

Below: Sturdy's not only hired out boats, punts and canoes, but also built their own. Here we see at work on a canoe (left to right) George Smith senior, George Smith junior (the ferryman) and Frank Sturdy, son of the founder. The firm was later taken over by Billy Henry, then sold to the Council in 1965.

Blenkhorn's boats were based on the landing stage near High Bridge, adjacent to the New Century Dining Rooms, so called because they were opened in 1900. The tall building was opened in 1906, as the High Bridge Private Hotel. This later view shows Blenkhorn's Boathouse Café, with day-trippers enjoying the river.

Winter snow did not prevent the essential work of maintaining the boats in a good state of repair. Here we see the proprietor, C.H. Blenkhorn, helped by Freddy Broad (right) who also worked for Henry's.

Left: Charles Hubert Blenkhorn, who died in 1966, as he could often be seen, in sailor's attire, busy splicing rope. Though the trade itself is seasonal both Knaresborough's boatlandings involved plenty of work like this behind the scenes.

Below: Dick Blenkhorn (left) took over the firm in 1966 and ran it until his own death in 1980. In the distance we can just make out a steam train crossing the viaduct.

In this 1930s view of the Market Place we see that the old central gas lamp has now been replaced by a less robust electric one. There is also a reminder that this was then the bus terminus. On the right is Mason's hardware store.

This terrace house, 3 Park Place, was a small sweets factory, that of Mr. & Mrs. H. Baines, seen here with their daughter Elsie, who in the war had served in Knaresborough as a postwoman and also in the Land Army. The photo is also of interest because it shows one of Knaresborough's splendid globe gas lamps. This one is now in Castle Museum in York.

This attractive river scene by Frank Newbould, looking towards Low Bridge, gives little indication of the industrial activity that took place on the left bank. Yet we can just see the gasworks set up in 1824 by the recently-formed body of Improvement Commissioners. The engineer was John Malam who, at a total cost of about £6,000, soon had a gas supply throughout the town. By 1841 there were 94 gas lamps, and by 1864 there were 129, making Knaresborough one of the earliest towns to have good street lighting. Next to the gas works was Joe Clough's soap factory, which later became a sheepskin rug factory.

Dobson's of Cheapside in 1907, based on the Nag's Head, the town's best-known provider of horse-drawn transport, including funeral carriages, ordered through this office. In the doorway are Mary Emma and Maude Warriner. To the left is J. H. Owen's, baker's and café.

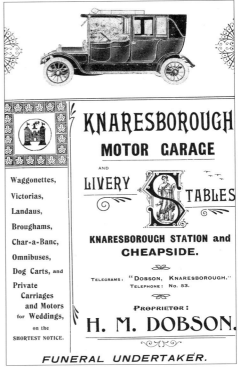

This Dobson's advertisement of 1914 is interesting to compare with a similar one printed in 1906 (see *Historic Knaresborough* page 74). Now we see that the big open carriage pulled by four horses has been replaced by this early motor car. Knaresborough was catching up with the times. By 1914 Britain already had 132,000 cars and 51,000 hackney cabs and omnibuses.

The successors of Dobson's were Dibbs's Taxis, formerly of Finkle Street, before being conveniently situated opposite the railway station. Here we see them lined up ready for the many people who in the 1950s still came to Knaresborough by train.

A reminder of an old Knaresborough trade, the tannery, and Clapham's garage, which for many years occupied these premises in York Road. The building has been used for other trades, including the manufacture of linen, but in 1984 the Old Tannery, as it is known, was restored and converted into flats.

Wally Gamble of Low Bond End, one of Knaresborough's almost forgotten characters from the 1930s. He combined two trades, that of roadsweeper and street musician, going round the town playing his tingalary or barrel-organ, which he pushed round on an old pram.

Billy Mudd plucking poultry at one of Knaresborough's long-established butcher's, Hutton's of Castlegate. Billy started work here in 1932 when he was 14, and stayed with Hutton's all his working life. He died in 1986.

Christmas is coming! An imposing display of turkeys and other birds, all plucked and cleaned by hand at the Waterside poultry factory founded here by Michael Burke in the 1930s. Poulterers have a long tradition in Knaresborough, including earlier firms such as those of Pullan, Carass, Taylor, Spence, Morris and Plummer. Mr Burke is standing in the centre, weighing a turkey.

Knaresborough Police Station, shortly before it was pulled down in 1968, when the police and magistrates' court moved to the old Council Offices in Gracious Street while rebuilding took place. At the door is Inspector R.W. McCollom, and on the left (in helmet) is P.C. Ted Harrower. Below them is Policewoman Helen Dunn, with Heather McCollom. Below the inspector is P.C. John Thornton. There to see the police station closed was Billy Mudd, the butcher, and the publican and customers from the nearby Castle Vaults.

three

Markets, Shops and Cafés

Cheapside in 1900, one of the main approaches to the Market Place, seen from its junction with the top of Briggate. A typical street scene of old Knaresborough, with a donkey cart, a milkman, women in shawls and aprons, and a man smoking a clay pipe. Beyond the hardware shop (right) is Hall's, 'Muffin and Crumpet Baker'. At the corner (left) is the 'Sixpence-Halfpenny Bazaar', where you could buy incandescent gaslights, clothes baskets and 'penny goods too numerous to mention' nothing costing more than sixpence-halfpenny.

The most noteworthy building in the Market Place is the Oldest Chemist's Shop in England, in continuous use as a pharmacy since at least 1720. The box windows on legs in the style of 'Chinese Chippendale' are thought to have been added in about 1760. Standing in the doorway are W.P. and E. Lawrence, father and son, whose combined service as chemists here spanned more than a hundred years.

Mr. Edmund Lawrence, still active in his nineties, at work in the Oldest Chemist's Shop, not long before his retirement in 1965. Here we see him working the pestle in a huge mortar used for pulverising ingredients. He would also proudly show other items from the apothecary's art: bleeding-couch, leech-jar, pill-making machine etc. The best known of the various Lawrence products was 'Ye Special Old Englyshe Lavender Water' made on the premises to a secret recipe.

The Market Place in about 1920, looking down Silver Street. Prominent is the gas lamp which had taken the place of the Market Cross since Victorian times. Propped up against the base of this are boards giving details of the bus service run by Brown's (five times a day between Knaresborough and Boroughbridge) who also advertised their 14 or 28 seater charabancs for 'pleasure parties'. The two ladies with bicycles are looking at the display of hams and sides of bacon outside Beal's grocer's. To the left is Mason's hardware and ironmonger's, and down Silver Street we can see the Hart's Horn inn (left) and Plummer's fishmonger's (right). The whole of the Market Place was cobbled at this time, and was not covered in tarmac until the early 1960s.

A busy market day in the post–war years before a stone cross replaced the lamp in 1953. Note also the gap at the far end, filled when the library was built in 1960, harmonising well with the surroundings.

Knaresborough Market in the 1960s, seen from the vantage-point of the newly-built library. All the shops at the far end have changed hands, but the general roof-line of the old Market Place remains remarkably unaltered.

The cattle market took possession of the High Street every Monday, and sometimes Tuesday as well, causing the considerable nuisance of obstruction and pollution, though the Improvement Commissioners in 1886 ordered the street to be cleared of muck and washed down at the end of each market. Eventually, in 1901, a special public meeting in the Town Hall discussed finding a permanent site, as well as other modernisations, such as bringing electricity to the town. A cattle market site was not, however, established until 1907.

Knaresborough Cattle Market, which was moved to a site between the Commmercial Hotel (now the Borough Bailiff) and Knaresborough Hospital, flourished for many years, the livestock now being kept in orderly pens. In this scene from the late 1940s we see Bill Wynn (holding the stick), with Cecil Holmes to his right.

G. HEBBLETHWAITE,
Drapery, Millinery, and Mantle
ESTABLISHMENT,
MARKET PLACE, KNARESBROUGH.

J. H. BOWLER, Practical Tailor.

Good Fit and Workmanship Guaranteed, at
moderate charges.
All the latest West End Styles,
And the choicest patterns to select from.

READY - MADE ::: DEPARTMENT.
The Largest and most selected Stock in this District
to choose from.
Our celebrated **10/6 Trousers**, ready-made
or to measure, are a marvel of Cheapness.
Boys' Suits from 1/11.
Men's Suits from 18/6.
Men's Trousers from 3/11.
We also keep a very large variety of Men's and
Boys' Cord and Mole Clothing.
Men's Cord and Mole Trousers from **3/6.**
Hats   Hats!   Hats!
If you want a fashionable Hat, at a reasonable price,
you must come to the Hatteries.
J. H. BOWLER, Market Place.
All the new shapes and shades kept in stock.   Agent
for all the leading manufacturers in the kingdom.
Our stock of Gents' Scarves, Collars, Fronts, Cuffs,
Braces, etc., is the best and most varied.
Note the Address:
J. H. BOWLER, The Hatteries,
Market Place, Knaresborough.

C. BENSON, Glass and Lead Merchant,
Plumber, Glazier and Gasfitter.
Dealer in all kinds of Iron Spouting.
✳ Hot and Cold Baths fitted up on the latest principle. ✳
**Finkle Street, Knaresboro', and
Green-Hammerton.**

Knaresborough 2

The aptly-named J.H. Bowler of 'The Hatteries', Market Place, was Knaresborough's best-known hatter, tailor and general clothier in Victorian and Edwardian times. Was he related to the London hatter, John Bowler, said to have originated the 'bowler hat' around 1850?

Knaresborough was well provided with retailers dealing in clothing. Along with Bowler's and Hebblethwaite's in the Market Place there was Fenton Bell's emporium, especially well-known for millinery. Originally on the site of Boot's, Fenton Bell's moved to the corner of Finkle Street and High Street, but was burnt down in 1941.

Thomas Stead, like Albert Holch below, achieved a remarkable double-act by combining the trade of a butcher with long and distinguished service on the Council. He was elected Chairman of the K.U.D.C. no less than thirteen times in succession (1904–1916) and in 1910 laid the foundation stone for the new Council offices in York Place.

Holch's pork butcher's, a first-class establishment with a long tradition, still maintained by the present firm of Robinson's. Soon after the First World War a pork butcher of German origin, George Holch, moved here from Castleford, taking over from H. Zisler, another German pork butcher. This photo from the 1920s shows the window abundantly stocked with pies, sausages, polony, black pudding, brawn, haslet, joints of pork and bacon. In the doorway stands young Albert Holch, the son, and his sister Lena. Albert was one of Knaresborough's best-known civic leaders, serving as Chairman of the K.U.D.C. six times, and being made an Alderman of the Harrogate District in 1974.

A Knaresborough shop photographed in 1898, graced by two ladies in fashionable Victorian dress, Mrs. Sarah Wheelhouse and her daughter Florence. Though licensed to sell ale and porter, as well as tobacco, William Wheelhouse, at the end of Church Lane, also sold sweets.

Opposite below: Another of Knaresborough's shoe shops and cobbler's was Harry Scruton's in High Street. His nephew, Sidney Clapham, is seen holding his eldest son, Frank. The shop was later taken over by George Hymas.

Right: Can you guess the date of this photo of Burton's, well-known fruit and vegetable shop in the Market Place? The poster advertising the Knaresborough Horticultural Show (examined on the original with a magnifying glass) gives his date as August, 1906. Burton's claimed to be the oldest-established seed shop in the district.

Knaresborough was once a town of little shops, with plenty of choice, including several sweet shops. Here is R. Lund's, with a row of jars of 'pure Swiss confectionery' and a window full of children's treats.

Above: The old firm of Brown's furnisher's, seen here in about 1905, a little further up High Street on the opposite side from Fred Brown's shop today. The man in the bowler is Benjamin Brown, later J.P., and Chairman of the Council (1925), who had set up business in Knaresborough in 1903. The firm's adverts regularly offered 'tons and tons of new and second-hand furniture'.

Left: Robinson's tobacconist's, High Street, (established in 1862) seen in about 1926. On the right is Henry Robinson, with his wife to the left. In the centre is their daughter, Aline, who later recalled how she loved selling snuff to the old men of Knaresborough. The neat window display included 'Gallaher's Irish Roll' – not bacon, but tobacco.

"Enchantment."

PARRS (Stationers) LTD.

HIGH STREET, KNARESBOROUGH,

Wireless Specialists.

Ask for one of our Complete Wireless Catalogues—Gratis.

Above: This advert from 1926 reminds us of the days when valve-sets and horn loud-speakers were still something of a novelty. Parr's, at a prominent corner leading from High Street to the Market Place, was the leading shop for newspapers, books and stationery, with a department selling wirelesses, cameras, pens and fancy goods.

Left: Abbott's, the popular greengrocer's, fruiterer's and florist's, which was founded in the 1890s by G.A. Abbott at 53 High Street, later moving to 43, where it remained till its closure in 1962.

Kit Horner, with his grandson, Sid, in about 1919. Kit was a stonemason and builder of fireplaces. He claimed he was the last man to be put in the Knaresborough stocks by a police sergeant tired of his practical jokes. Sid Horner became a photographer, with a shop in Cheapside (now occupied by Vollans Photography) and later a printer.

Right: The Mudds of Cheapside were one of the town's best-known families. Especially popular was Florrie Mudd, here seen outside her sweetshop with her mother, Alice Mudd, who lived to the age of 94. Many a Knaresborough child has come here to spend a 'Saturday penny' – and more!

Opposite above: The interior of the family grocer's, Dinsdale's in the Market Place (now Heapy's), as many will remember it, with old-style scales, bacon-slicer, coffee-grinder etc., and everything personally cut, weighed and wrapped. The wonderful aroma lingers on in our memories, but this traditional grocer's, founded in 1849, closed down in 1965.

Opposite below: A particularly attractive shop, at the corner of High Street and Station Road, was Ken Crowther's greengrocer's, with its open-air displays of fruit and vegetables, seen here with Mr. and Mrs. Crowther in attendance. Formerly this was the Red Lion inn.

SHIPLEY'S

Riverside Cafe and Tea Gardens

(Opposite Sturdy's Boats).

KNARESBOROUGH

PARTIES CATERED FOR.

Prices on Application.

LUNCHEONS   HIGH TEAS   NOTED ICE CREAM
TOBACCO & CONFECTIONERY

Phone **3277** K'boro   **Entrance near foot of Castle Steps**

ii

Providing refreshments for day-trippers on Waterside was Shipley's, noted for its ice cream, in the early days all churned by hand. From about 1922 until 1945 Shipley's café was a mecca for visitors, who poured into Knaresborough in their hundreds, mostly from railway excursions.

The entrance to Castle Yard, showing Haley's sweetshop on the right and the Castle Café on the left. In the distance we can just make out the old bandstand of the 1930s, built close to the remains of the Castle wall.

The Old Town Hall, built in 1862 on the site of the old Sessions House, which had two prison cells underneath. From this balcony speeches were made by candidates seeking election as Knaresborough's two M.P.s. The custom of the Town Mayor speaking from the balcony during the popular open-air carol service was started by the author in 1979.

Spencer's Town Hall Café, started here in 1920 by John William Spencer, was a Knaresborough institution for almost 70 years. More recently managed by his son, Harold, it served meals to thousands of visitors, especially coach parties, as well as hosting wedding receptions, dinners and dances.

On the opposite side of the Market Place from Spencer's Café was another popular venue, the Tudor Café. Though the frontage we see here is a later reconstruction, much of the building is genuinely Tudor, so the name was justified. For many years before alterations in about 1930 this was Hebblethwaite's, the draper's.

The interior of the Tudor Café had an old-world atmosphere, partly the result of its oak beams. It was also one of many old buildings in the town reputed to be haunted. The trilby hats, like the car parked outside, were typical of the leisurely pre-war days.

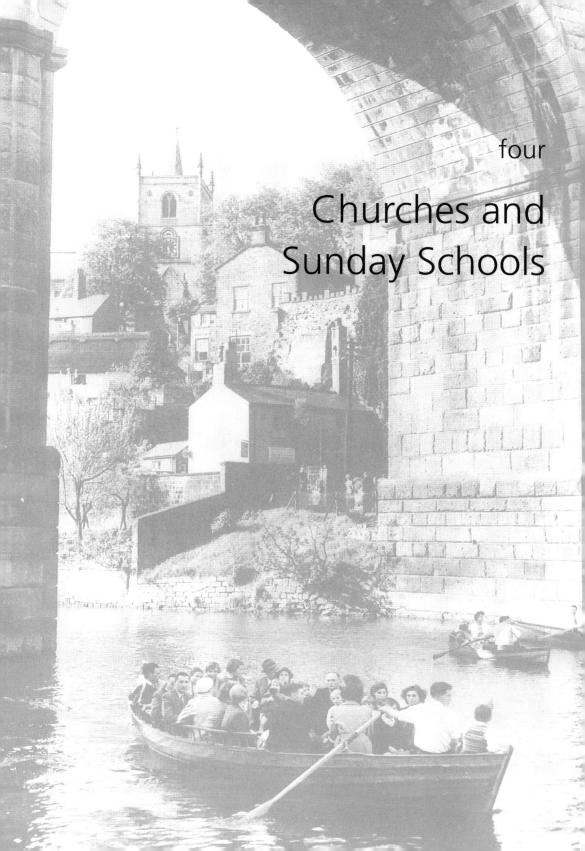

four

Churches and
Sunday Schools

Above: The beautiful Parish Church of St. John the Baptist, photographed in 1936. In the foreground are some of the old gravestones, half hidden by long grass and enclosed by railings, all altered when the churchyard was landscaped in 1973. The name of Kirkgate, leading down to the church, suggests a pre-Norman site, but the first documentary reference was in 1114. The west end we see here was completed during Queen Philippa's restoration of 1343.

Left: The Tudor font of St. John's, with the late Jacobean cover suspended from its wrought-iron bracket. The font cover was once locked into position to prevent the holy water of baptism from being stolen for the purposes of witchcraft.

Looking through to the Slingsby Chapel, we see the columns and arches as they looked towards the end of the fifteenth century. The pulpit, near the south-west pier of the tower, stood here until 1978, when it was removed during alterations to the crossing area.

The old Parish Church, with its distinctive miniature spire (dating from around 1520), can be seen from many enjoyable viewpoints on the river, as in this photo, looking through an arch of the viaduct, with a pleasure-boat in the foreground. The church tower is also unusual because above the clock are inscribed the words 'Redeeming the Time', a phrase used twice by St. Paul to exhort the best possible use of the time we have left.

An outstanding worker in the Church of England was Miss Margaret Collins of Swadforth House, Gracious Street. In 1872 she presented the reredos, a fine representation of the Last Supper in Caen stone, to St. John's, and in 1905 donated the archway leading to Holy Trinity. Active on the Ladies Visiting Committee, she was, till her death in 1922, a familiar sight in Knaresborough, going round with a basket, distributing food to the poor and needy.

The bells of St. John's as seen in October 1925, ready to be hung after recasting. The peal of eight was originally installed in 1774 by the Revd Thomas Collins. Made by Peake and Chapman of London, they weighed a total of 76 hundredweight and cost £462. 3s., with additional expense for 'wharfage, shipping, freight, insurance', as well as hanging. Here the bells are presided over by (left) the Vicar, Canon H.L. Ogle and the Parish Clerk, Charles Inman.

This 1930s view of the way into Knaresborough down Bland's Hill shows the prominent position of Holy Trinity, built in 1856 at a cost of £2,800, Knaresborough's second Parish Church. Its spire reaches a height of 166 feet, making it a landmark for many miles around.

The choir of Holy Trinity in about 1930. In the centre (in white) is Joe Morley, organist and choirmaster. To his left is Joseph Barker, churchwarden. To his right are the Revd Downes, Canon Hartley and Henry Eddy, churchwarden.

St. Mary's Roman Catholic Church, Bond End, as it looked during a service for first Holy Communion in the days before the church interior was redesigned in 1973. The building dates from 1831, Catholics having worshipped at the mission off Briggate, now demolished.

The contrasting simplicity of the Primitive Methodist Chapel in High Street, built in 1901 as a successor to the old 1854 chapel off the top of Briggate. Both these premises have had commercial uses, the one seen here being a household furnisher's. The term 'Primitive' referred to the desire to return to the original fervour of Methodism, as distinct from the more formal style of the Wesleyans.

The choir of St. John's in 1956, when the organist and choirmaster was Brian Dockray, who also taught at Castle Boys School. The men (from left) are Billy Wilde, Harry Butterfield, John Wilson, Ernest Smith, Brian Dockray, Gordon Halliday, Harry Colley, Fred Herrington, Eric Cosgrove, Neil De Lacey, behind whom is Mr. Bristow, the verger.

The choir in about 1964, soon after Harry Colley had taken over as organist and choirmaster. On the front row is the Vicar, the Revd M.R.J. Manktelow, with the Curate, the Revd R. Capstick, on his right, and on his left, Jim Binks, church treasurer, lay reader and the town's 'kidcatcher' (attendance officer). Harry Colley, who was also headmaster of Castle Boys School, is on the extreme right.

A happy group of Sunday School children and teachers from the Knaresborough Congregational Church, taken during a picnic in the 1920s. The Congregational Church (now the United Reformed Church) first worshipped in a thatched barn on Windsor Lane in 1697, with chapels later built on the same site.

Children in the 1930s ready to dance round the maypole on the stage of the Congregational Sunday School – just one example of the many activities that were organised alongside Christian teaching in the town's Sunday Schools.

Right: The gifted draughtsman, Albert Walker, at work recording another of Knaresborough's old buildings. Alas, many of those seen in his drawings from the 1940s and 50s have been demolished or greatly altered.

Below: The elegant spire of the Congregational Church, built in 1865, is seen in this view of Gracious Street by Albert Walker, drawn in 1949. Though the Methodist Church and Holy Trinity are also in this vicinity the name 'gracious' has nothing to do with churches, and is derived from the Anglo-Saxon for 'houses along the ditch'.

GRACIOUS STREET, KNARESBOROUGH

A WALKER /49

The Methodist Chapel (1815), the oldest building (after St. John's) still in use as a place of worship. Methodism flourished in Knaresborough following several visits by John Wesley, and this was the first real chapel, as distinct from a meeting-house (still sound, in spite of the tilting caused by a wide-angle lens). Once known as the 'Waterloo Chapel', because it was built in the year of the famous battle, it was a well-attended place of worship, with a capacity of 800, until the Victorian chapel (1868) was opened on the adjacent site. The year it was built the chapel became the head of a far-flung country circuit, which included chapels in Harrogate and Wetherby. Over the years it has housed the pioneering Sabbath and Day School, run by Methodists (with around 170 scholars), and later the army, during both world wars, and the West Riding secondary school, before it moved down to Stockwell Road. It has also been used for the Sunday School, a wide variety of social occasions, and as a polling station.

A gathering on 4 June, 1903 for the stone-laying of the new Methodist Chapel in Park Grove, Scriven. This was only two years after the opening of the Primitive Methodist Chapel in High Street, and indicated a considerable Methodist population in Knaresborough at the beginning of the century. The census of 1851 had shown 843 Methodists, 2,047 Anglicans, 227 Congregationalists and 250 Roman Catholics.

Local preachers of the Knaresborough Methodist Circuit photographed in 1907. Based on the Gracious Street chapel, they rode out on horseback to take services in town and country chapels, the horse being provided free, unless the distance was under seven miles, in which case the preacher often walked there and back. These tough circuit-riders were carrying on the tradition of John Wesley, who had first preached in Knaresborough in 1742.

Park Grove Methodist Chapel in 1907, three years after its opening, with a group of Sunday School children and their teachers. Opposite the chapel at 12 Park Grove lived Philip Inman, later Lord Inman, who was for a time a member of this Sunday School.

The laying of bricks (1935) for the Sunday School built next to Park Grove Methodist Church. Seen laying a brick is Ernest Wetherill, with John Hogg (in the cap) next to him. Also looking on are a guide and members of the Girls' League. Behind the boys is Alfred Phillipson and Ernest Alton, J.P. (in trilby), with the foreman of Birch's checking the bricklaying.

A gathering of Methodists at Park Grove to celebrate the 50th chapel anniversary in 1954. The group includes two long-serving ministers, the Revd Samuel Hulton (back row, fifth from left) and the Revd W. Herbert Alton (left, middle row). The guest speaker had been Lord Inman.

A celebration in Gracious Street Sunday School of 150 years of Methodism on the site, with Mr. and Mrs. J. Kenn cutting a cake in the shape of the now-demolished 1868 chapel. Johnny Kenn had for many years been associated with the well-known grocer's, Kenn and Townsley, next door to the chapel.

Children of Gracious Street Methodist Sunday School in the 1960s standing in front of the Victorian chapel, pulled down and replaced in 1975. Amongst the adults at the back can be seen (from the left) Derek Wilkinson and Horace Hill, and (third from the right) Wilf Masheder.

Ready with their little baskets of fruit for the 1967 Harvest Festival at Gracious Street Methodist Church are two of the author's children, Tim and Ann.

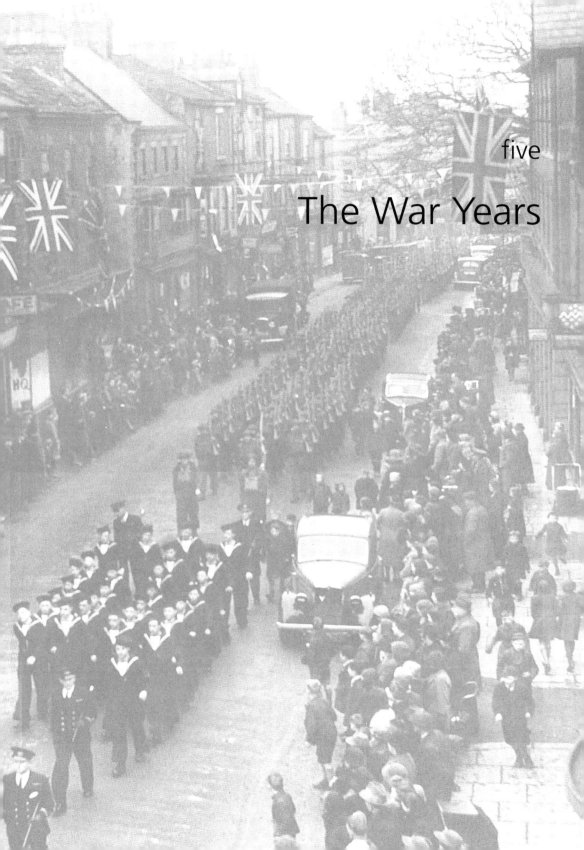

five

The War Years

A salute for the fallen, fired at Knaresborough Cemetery. A total of 156 men from Knaresborough were killed in action during the First World War, and the years between 1914 and 1918 brought untold misery to this town, as everywhere else.

A cavalryman of the First World War, just one of the many hundreds of Knaresborough men who volunteered to serve their country. He was Charles Anderson, who trained at York with the Yorkshire Dragoons. Attached to the Scots Grays, he went to France and was in action at Ypres and on the Somme, being promoted to sergeant. His horse (which had come second in the Grand National of 1912) was killed, but Sergeant Anderson, though gassed, wounded and buried alive by a shell, lived to tell the tale, returning as the only survivor of his troop.

Outside Knaresborough House in 1915 we see the band of the Royal Scots Grays, in Knaresborough to give a concert to raise money for the war effort. The regiment had a close connection with the town through their Commanding Officer, Colonel William Fellowes Collins, D.S.O., who gave distinguished service to Knaresborough in peace and war, becoming Chairman of the K.U.D.C. in 1924, as well as chairman of magistrates. Also in the front row (from left) are William Elbourne, organist and choirmaster of St. John's, Lady Evelyn Collins and the Vicar, Canon W.E. Hancock. The officer with the moustache is Major Archie Collins and at the end of the row is Bandmaster Frayling.

Knaresborough Hospital in about 1916, when it was used as a military hospital for convalescent servicemen. In the centre is Lady Evelyn Collins, then serving as Matron. The physician seen here is Dr. I.D. Mackay, one of Knaresborough's two general practitioners, the other being Dr. W.J. Forbes.

Peace celebrations following the end of the 'Great War' of 1914–1918, with jubilant crowds thronging the Market Place. This was where the populace always congregated for any special public occasion, such as Queen Victoria's Golden Jubilee and the Coronation of George V. The scene is the afternoon of Friday 18 July, 1919, when the children assembled before being given a tea-party and sports events. All the girls and women are in their best dresses and hats. The man addressing the crowd is Councillor H. Eddy, J.P. This is one of several surviving early pictures taken by the High Street photographer, S. Wilkinson.

An interesting view which combines the old Russian cannon with the new war memorial. The cannon (right), presented to the town in 1857 after being captured at Sebastopol in the Crimean War, was used for firing harmless charges of turf out across the river, until it was taken for salvage in the Second War. The war memorial, seen here soon after its installation in 1921, had an elegant top, but in this exposed position it was blown down, and was replaced by the present stubbier cross in the 1930s.

A procession on the way to an Armistice Day service soon after the First World War. The men are marching into Gracious Street past the Council Offices, with Birnand Hall in the background. Ever since those days annual services of remembrance, organised by the British Legion, have been reverently observed by the town.

The Auxiliary Fire Service in 1941, assembled outside King James's Grammar School, and ready to cope with any enemy action. Fortunately there were few demands made on the service, though on one occasion the Germans did drop bombs on Knaresborough in the area of Scriven Hall, which they may have been aiming at. The central figure (not in uniform) in this 'Dad's Army' photo is 'Prof' Geoffrey Watson, head of music at King James's.

Digging for victory during the Second World War. Potatoes are being prepared for storage in a clamp by children of Knaresborough Secondary School. They had grown them in their 'War Garden', nearly an acre taken from the playing fields at Haya Park.

Warship Week (21–28 March, 1942) united the whole of Knaresborough in a special war effort. Sir Harold Mackintosh had arranged for the town to adopt H.M.S. *Wallflower*, a corvette used for convoy escorts and anti-submarine work. This was on condition that the town raised at least £100,000 through National Savings. Here we see the townsfolk lining High Street to welcome the opening procession, which included Sea Cadets, a contingent from the King's Regiment, A.T.S., W.A.A.F., Home Guard, R.A.F. etc. Warship Week was one of the most successful projects ever undertaken in Knaresborough. The target of £100,000 was reached in three days, and by the end of the week the town had raised £337,712, equivalent to more than £41 per head. This was the highest in the whole of England, beating Ilkley's £38 per head, for example.

KNARESBOROUGH

Sweeps up the Nazi!

During Warship Week
INVEST ALL
YOU POSSIBLY
CAN IN

3% SAVINGS BONDS
2½% NATIONAL WAR BONDS
3% DEFENCE BONDS
SAVINGS CERTIFICATES &
INCREASE your DEPOSITS
in the POST OFFICE
SAVINGS BANK and
COUNTY SAVINGS BANK.

MOTHER SHIPTON had her "intuitions" —sound ones too according to tradition. But Hitler's intuitions entirely overlook the resolute spirit of the British people. Everywhere we are building or adopting fighting ships to sweep away the Nazi menace for good and all. Yes, we'll make a clean sweep of it this time!

KNARESBOROUGH, like every town and city in the Kingdom, now puts its hand to the task. Everyone appreciates the urgency of the task and everyone will do his best to place Knaresborough high in the magnificent record of Warship Weeks.

Full details from your Bank, Building Society, Selling Centres, Post Office, Stockbroker, or Savings Group.

KNARESBOROUGH WARSHIP WEEK
MARCH 21-28

Issued by the Knaresborough Warship Week Committee.

Left: Even Mother Shipton was enlisted in Warship Week. In this advert she is sweeping away Hitler, with a picture of the corvette the town was aiming to adopt.

Below: As the W.A.A.F march through the Market Place in Warship Week the salute is taken by Rear Admiral the Hon. L. Forbes–Sempill.

A Warship Week crowd of young people, with Knaresborough Girl Guides in the foreground. They had gathered in the Castle Grounds to take part in community singing and to see the huge thermometer target which had been set by Viscountess Snowden, and was adjusted each day as the money came in. The faces seem to indicate real interest in the proceedings, and the sense of unity that the war years engendered.

The crowd assembled on 21 March, 1942, in front of Castle Boys School, on the wall of which was the thermometer indicating progress towards the Warship Week target. In front of this is a platform on which are the Rear Admiral who had taken the salute, Sir Harold and Lady Mackintosh and Lady Snowden. Standing in front are Sea Cadets and the R.A.F. band.

Councillor Ernest Beaumont, Chairman of the Council, announcing the final Warship Week figure, the highest in the whole of England per head of population. Next to the almost bursting thermometer is a painting of the now-adopted H.M.S. *Wallflower*. Also on the front row (right) are Colonel W.F. and Lady Evelyn Collins. Sir Harold Mackintosh was detained by urgent War Savings business in London, but a special telegram was sent to the people of Knaresborough, reading: 'Have just heard magnificent result of your campaign and hasten to send my heartiest congratulations. Signed, A.V. Alexander, First Lord of the Admiralty.'

Scriven Hall, once the home of the Slingsby family, played an important part during the Second World War, when the hall and its extensive grounds were used for training involving tanks, artillery and Scottish regiments. What actually took place there was top secret, but the hall was important enough to have been visited by Churchill. Later the grounds were used as a centre for prisoners of war. Scriven Hall was destroyed by fire in 1952.

Another Knaresborough contribution to the war effort was this parachute factory in Iles Lane, which had formerly been a shirt factory. Parachutes were also made in the former Claro Laundry on Waterside, where they specialised in parachutes for star shells.

Knaresborough Army Cadets, followed by Air Cadets, marching down Park Row in 1943. The first cadet seen here is Ken Frost, behind him P. Jackson, G. Pitchford, A. Elliot, C. Tipling, R. Roberts, S. Dodds, F. Hustwith, T. Raine-Ellerker, L. Parsons, R. Mountain, H. Whorley and D. Hutson. The two boys marching alongside are Ronnie Darvill (left) and Terry Smith.

A ceremony in July, 1943 during which bugles and drums were presented to Knaresborough Army Cadets by Lord Harewood, who had in 1942 given a County Flag, which was presented to Knaresborough for the record achievement of Warship Week and was flown from the battlements of the Castle.

An end-of-the-war party organised by Mrs. Edith Cleasby, standing to the left of the girl playing the accordion. Mrs. Cleasby, who worked for the Red Cross, was one of numerous local people who did voluntary war work.

A meeting in Scriven Hall at which returned prisoners-of-war are saying thank-you to Mrs. Edith Cleasby, Red Cross parcels organiser.

A V.E. Day street party to celebrate the end of the war (8 May, 1945) organised by local people on land between Stockwell Grove and Stockwell Drive.

A typical Remembrance Day service in the years following the Second World War, in which 54 Knaresborough men had lost their lives. Conducted here by the Revd R.A. Talbot, who had been awarded the Military Cross, this increasingly well–attended service includes the laying of wreaths and the two minutes' silence in a setting which has both the military association of Knaresborough Castle and the peaceful sound of the river below.

Thanksgiving Week, ending on 6 October, 1945, was another campaign to increase National Savings, still needed to pay war debts. Opening the week is Major-General C.M. Smith of Northern Command. To the left of the microphone is Sir Harold Mackintosh.

The highlight of Thanksgiving Week was a German V2 long-range rocket, the kind of flying-bomb which caused such havoc towards the end of the war. This one weighed 12 tons and travelled at 3,000 m.p.h. Here we see it on display in Castle Yard, with the Dispensary in the background. Knaresborough rounded off its outstanding results in Warship Week, Wings for Victory and Salute the Soldier campaigns, with another excellent total of £243,171.

six

Recreation and Sports

Knaresborough has always known how to enjoy itself. Here we see an early outing setting off in front of the Elephant and Castle at the top of High Street. The wagonette had probably been hired from Richmond's Stables, York Road, and the trip was one of many excursions organised by the town's pubs, clubs and churches.

Knaresborough Boy Scouts, soon after Baden-Powell's launching of the movement in 1907. They are wearing the characteristic hats, neckerchiefs, and lanyards attached to a whistle, and one is holding the patrol flag. The thatched cottage to the left was the birthplace of Philip Inman, later Lord Inman of Knaresborough, in Water Bag Bank, now replaced by a modern Tudor Cottage, marked by a plaque.

Right: John Patrick, the long-serving postman, one of Knaresborough's first scoutmasters, wearing medals awarded for service in the Boer War and First World War. Note the scoutmaster's hat, a style borrowed from South Africa by Baden-Powell, of whom this portrait reminds us. Mr. Patrick, who died in 1929, had the honour of being spoken to by King George V, who was on a visit to Goldsborough Hall in 1923 and stopped when he saw his medals.

Below: A long-serving scoutmaster of more recent years was W.H. (Bill) Campbell, who led Knaresborough Scouts from 1952 to 1975, and was awarded the Silver Acorn for his work in 1994. Here we see him with Cubs and Scouts at a St. George's Day parade in 1954.

All Visitors to Knaresborough ❦ ❦ and Neighbourhood

Should not fail in visiting the far-famed . . . . .

Dropping Well

Unmounted .
Views, . .
Medallions, .
Cabinets, and
Opalines, . .
In Various Sizes.

A Large . .
Collection of
Petrifactions
on View . .
and for Sale.

It is noted for its Petrifying Properties and surroundings of Magnificent Scenery.

ENTRANCE AT LOW BRIDGE. ❦ Mrs. COMER, Lessee.

The remarkable petrifactions of the Dropping Well were first described by John Leland in 1540. He made no mention of Mother Shipton, nor does this advert in a guidebook of 1906.

A pair of daring stilt-walkers from Bertram Mills going round publicising the circus, which would be held in a field on Crag Top, off Aspin Lane. Barratt's and other circuses also visited the town, adding to a variety of open-air entertainment that included German bands, dancing bears and band concerts. This scene in front of the Knaresborough Café in High Street (at one time known as Ellerker's) looks as though it is from the late 1930s.

By this time, just before the First World War, horse-drawn wagonettes were being replaced by charabancs, as on this outing organised by the Cross Keys, complete with uniformed chauffeur. The vehicle actually belonged to the Harrogate Road Car Company.

Boys in a pre-First World War concert-party organised by Miss Isabelle Phillipson, a keen Methodist of Scriven, who raised money for charitable purposes through these concerts, all typical of the days of home-made entertainment.

Another group from Miss Phillipson's concert party, performing the song 'We are grandmothers old every one'. Mrs. Marjorie Cooper (formerly Johnson), who was in this group, tells me they raised £29, which paid for a boy to be looked after in a children's home for a whole year.

Pirates of Penzance, performed at the Oddfellows' Hall in the 1920s, when the popularity of Gilbert and Sullivan operettas was at its height. The Oddfellows' Hall often served as Knaresborough's theatre, and was also used for the showing of silent films at this time, later sound films, when it was called the Roxy Cinema, popularly known as the 'bug-hutch'.

The principals of a performance of *The Mikado* given at Knaresborough Town Hall in 1923. This was one of the productions staged by the concert-party run by Mrs. Hearne, who lived on Waterside. Second from the right is Peep Bo, played by Marjorie Johnson of Richmond House, Waterside.

A 1922 production of Edward German's *Tom Jones* featured Jim Smith and Marjorie Johnson. This picture suggests that the amateur dramatics at the time was of a high standard.

A Cinderella from the early 1920s, played by Bessie Whitehouse in a performance of the pantomime staged at Knaresborough Congregational Sunday School.

Punting was a popular pastime on the Nidd during the first half of the century, especially in the quieter parts near Bilton Fields, seen here..

This anonymous photographer should have been complimented on the excellent composition of his picture, as well as the presence of mind which led him to take it. There is surely no posing here. And what was one lady saying to the other? And what was the cow thinking?

Boating on the Nidd in 1937. The stretch of river extending from the rapids near Conyngham Hall down to the weir by Castle Mill has always been popular with residents, no less than visitors. Whether simply 'messing about in boats' or being taken on guided pleasure-boat cruises by George Smith, there was always lovely scenery and historical interest on both banks of the river. The relaxed atmosphere on the river itself sometimes contrasted with that on Waterside, packed with excursion crowds every sunny weekend.

Knaresboro Working Men's Club and Institute.

Above: The rare treat of skating on the frozen River Nidd, as seen here in 1947. This has happened several times, the earliest within living memory being in the unusually severe winter of 1929.

Left: Knaresborough Working Men's Club, overlooking the river from its enviable position at 25 Kirkgate. It had moved here from higher up, at No. 6, as the Trades and Labour Club, in 1925. By this time Knaresborough also had a Conservative and a Liberal Club and several Friendly Societies.

Knaresborough Cricket Club in about 1891, a photograph by the organist and choirmaster, George Arnold. In 1891 the Club was already venerable, having been founded in 1815, the year of Waterloo, making it one of the oldest in Yorkshire, with a fine reputation, especially in the mid-nineteenth century. The Club first had grounds at the top of Aspin Lane in 1863. Then, in 1964, these grounds were exchanged for the present Crag Top site which had been King James's Grammar School's playing fields.

More than half a century later the Knaresborough Cricket Club first XI on 14 July, 1950, the occasion of a benefit match for Frank Prentice. A regular player with the First Eleven from the age of sixteen, Frank was recruited by Herbert Sutcliffe to play with distinction for Leicestershire.

Knaresborough Forest Cricket Club photographed on 6 September, 1952, with Bill Linden (captain) holding the cup. Starting out as the Knaresborough Liberal Club team, they moved in the late 1940s to the cricket field behind the Union Inn, previously used by the Calcutt Cricket Club. The groundsman, Mr. Hardcastle, is on the right, next to Billy Martin, a foundermember.

Knaresborough Junior Football Club in 1936. The players, back row, left to right: are 'Sonny' Lund, Fred Malthouse, Harold Ascough, William Robinson, William Porter, Wilfred Broadbelt. Sitting, from left: Kenneth Broadbelt, Keith Brown, Eric Dobson, Sam Young, Geoff Outhwaite (Captain) and George Pedal. The adult organisers are Mr. and Mrs. Albion Hudson.

Knaresborough Football Club, though started much later than the Cricket Club, was a going concern from the early 1900s, when Major (later Colonel) W.F. Collins was president and Frank Sturdy chairman, with headquarters at the Marquis of Granby. This team, 'the Rovers', from the 1950/51 season is front, from left: Outing, Holmes, Gibson, Waite, James. Back, from left: Raper, Raine-Ellerker, Carne, Whincup, Ewing, Conway.

A homely cup of tea in the Veterans Club in October 1953. Lord Inman (left) is chatting to Mr. Richard Simpson, aged 94. At the back (left) is Bill Ryder.

Knaresborough Silver Band in 1950, a photograph presented to Mr. S. Coupland 'in recognition of his long and valuable services as Friend and Conductor.' On his right is Councillor Albert Holch. The band was first known as the Volunteer Band, then the Prize Band and the Brass Band, before becoming well-established as the Silver Band. The members are seen here in their new uniforms.

The Knaresborough Darby and Joan Club celebrating its fourth birthday in 1954, with a visit from the Chairman of the K.U.D.C., Councillor Charles Cooper and Councillor H. Knutton. Cutting the cake is Mrs. F. Sims, aged 85. Holding the flowers is Mrs. R. Chew.

Knaresborough's 'Donkey Man', the popular Yorkshire character David Allott, seen here soon after he started in 1955, with his donkeys and enthusiastic helpers. For nearly forty years Mr. Allott's twenty or so donkeys gave pleasure to visitors and residents alike, with rides along Bilton Fields (sixpence in old money) and in Donkey Derbys, raising considerable sums for charity. At David Allott's funeral in 1993 it was a moving experience to see one of his beloved donkeys pulling a donkey-cart bearing his coffin. Visitors strolling along Waterside in the post-war years could have their picture taken by 'Charlie', a familiar character who had his stand near the Viaduct.

Opposite above: Visitors strolling along Waterside in the post-war years could have their picture taken by 'Charlie', a familiar character who had his stand near the Viaduct.

Opposite below: Garden parties held by the churches have for many years been regular summer events. This hoop-la scene from the St. John's Parish Church Garden Party in June 1958 shows the Vicar, the Revd W.A. Talbot, and the Chairman, Councillor A.W. Haddon. Looking on are Christine and Barry Hutchins. The event raised £120. St. Mary's Garden Party the following month raised £201 towards the new Catholic school.

Amateur dramatics has been an important part of Knaresborough's social life, in recent years centred on the Knaresborough Players, with their own 'little theatre' (formerly the Elephant and Castle ballroom), the Fraser Theatre. In the early years they performed in Holy Trinity Hall, for example, as in this 1963 Old Time Music Hall, with Ken Nowell holding the basket. Next to him are Gladys Nowell, Dorothy Anderton and Eileen Cosgrove, with Rachel Oliphant and Diane Annakin at the back.

A performance by the Knaresborough Players in 1964 of *King of the Castle* at the Community Centre. Pictured front: Bill Hardacre, Gladys Nowell, Betty Cosgrove, Dorothy Anderton. At the back are Ken Nowell, M. McDonald, Eileen Cosgrove, Brian Cosgrove, Harold Stocks.

seven

Special
Occasions

Knaresborough Market Place has traditionally been the hub of every public celebration, the old gas lamp serving as a focal point and support for bunting. Why are the flags out on this occasion? The photo has no date or details, but comparison with similar photos identifies this as the 22 June, 1911, the Coronation of George V, and the day would feature, as in the case of Queen Victoria's Jubilee, what Knaresborough people called 'the rejoicings'.

The famous houseboat, the Marigold, which was not only a delightful Edwardian café, but an essential feature of special occasions on the river, mainly the Water Carnivals held each August. Owned by the O'Reilly sisters, the Marigold was usually moored at a point between Castle Mill and Sturdy's Landing, but it moved to take a central place in the carnivals, when it was festooned in coloured lights and had a band playing on the upper deck.

Above: The handsome evergreen oak planted by Sir Charles Slingsby on the village green of Scriven when he came of age in 1845. Though there are worthy memorials to him in St. John's Parish Church (the effigy on his tomb and the west window) it is to be hoped that this unique living memorial will survive. Though felled because of disease in 1996, one of the saplings taken from it will provide a continuing oak on Scriven Green.

Left: Sir Charles Slingsby, photographed in the 1860s, characteristically holding a hunting whip. This portrait must have been taken only a short time before his tragic death on 4 February, 1869, when he was drowned during a fox-hunt. The ferryboat carrying the hunt across the River Ure near Newby Hall capsized, resulting in the death by drowning of six men and eight horses.

Part of the audience for the Knaresborough Water Carnival in the early 1900s, looking down on the river from vantage-points below the Castle and from rows of wooden seats (supplied by Kitchen's) above Sturdy's Landing. They would see, for example, the procession of decorated boats led by the 'Fairy Queen of the Carnival' or stunts such as Don Pedro walking across the gorge on a tightrope and pushing a wheelbarrow. On floating platforms of punts or boats tied together were pierrots, glee choirs and other musicians. At night there were myriads of fairylights (for years all set up by George Smith) and fireworks raining down from the viaduct in a spectacular 'Niagara Falls'.

In the years before the First World War the Tradesmen's Processions in June were colourful occasions, with decorated carts celebrating different aspects of the life of the town. Coming down High Street we see the old fire engine of 1774, followed by the Fire Brigade. Behind the spectators is the newly-built Primitive Methodist Chapel (1901).

This view of the Tradesmen's Procession is of interest because it shows, on the extreme right, Wintringham Hall. Once connected with Sir Edward Plumpton and Joan Wintringham, and in living memory a well-known High Street café, this was one of Knaresborough's oldest houses, inexcusably demolished in 1960.

Above: Leading this Tradesmen's Procession of 1909 is a soldier on horseback, followed by a marching band. The view down Cheapside is of interest, partly because of the dress of the school-children running alongside the procession, and partly because of the establishments that can be identified by their signs. On the left, past the 6 Qw d bazaar, is F. Hardcastle's cycle shop; at the far end is the Castle Café, and on the right is the sign of F. Tipling, the well-known chimney sweep.

Opposite above: The Tradesmen's Procession of 1909 continues with horse-drawn carriages, this one belonging to Pickersgill's, the High Street grocer's, which advertised itself as 'the economical tea establishment . . . a trial solicited'.

Opposite below: Passing through the Market Place this part of the Tradesmen's Procession features a giant pushball, which was to be used in a contest in the evening. The shops in the background include (left) the shoeshop of Henry Eddy, well-known Councillor. At the left-hand corner are the Leeds Dining Rooms, popular with cyclists. To the right of this the magnifying glass reveals suffragettes holding a banner with the words 'Votes for Women'.

Here a local dairyman, L. Wilkins, is preparing to take part in the Tradesmen's Procession. He was very proud of his pet cow, as we see from the picture below.

The Wilkins cow takes its place in the procession, a symbol of quality in the days when the milkman came round in his cart and ladled out fresh milk into the waiting jug.

Princess Mary, the Princess Royal, of Goldsborough Hall, opening a new wing at Knaresborough Hospital on 4 August, 1925. With her is the Master of the Workshouse, Mr. Harper, his wife and children. Second from left is Benjamin Brown, Chairman of the Council.

The Princess Royal, patron of the Red Cross, at Conyngham Hall, during the period when it was used as a convalescent home for servicemen around the time of the Second War.

The official opening of the Fysche Hall playing fields on 2 September, 1929, by Lady Evelyn Collins, O.B.E., J.P., who later became Chairman of the Knaresborough Urban District Council and of the governors of King James's Grammar School. With her is Councillor Robert Holmes. 'Fysche' Hall, by the way, was an unfortunate attempt to give an air of antiquity to the original spelling of Fish Hall.

The official opening of the Moat Gardens on 2 July, 1931 by Councillor William Wright, Chairman of the Housing and Town Improvement Committee, here seen addressing a crowd which includes children from the Castle Schools.

As part of the official opening of the Moat Gardens a crowd gathers round the new paddling pool, seen here in its pastoral setting above meadows along the River Nidd.

The paddling pool in the Moat Gardens being given a first trial by children of the town in July 1931. After town twinning in 1969 the name of the park was changed to Bebra Gardens.

Jim Kell, the 'Carnival King', presiding over the 1936 Coronation of the Knaresborough Carnival Queen. Jim provided a link between the Water Carnival and the many street carnivals he organised for charity, often with a Christian theme, such as 'The Rock of Ages'. His beautifully-decorated floats and tableaux were legendary, and paved the way for later carnival events such as Children's Day. The royal party here consists of Terry Wood, Miss Smith, Vera Clark, Joe Stockburn, Miss Irene Skelton (Queen), Miss Harker, Miss Jewitt, Miss G. Wilkinson, Brian Jordan.

Opposite above: The Silver Jubilee of the accession of King George and Queen Mary was commemorated, for example, on 6 May, 1935 by the planting of this tree on the village green at Old Scriven. Holding the spade is Sir Algernon Firth of Scriven Hall (and Firth's Carpets). Lady Firth is in the wheelchair. Holding the tree is Herbert Titley, head gardener from 1928 to 1936.

Opposite below: A Silver Jubilee group at the Knaresborough Council School in 1935, which the following year became the Knaresborough Secondary Modern School. This photo was taken by Arthur Prest, who gave each child a copy to include in a specially-designed Jubilee folder.

Left: The Jubilee Fountain, bought by public subscription to commemorate Queen Victoria's Jubilee in 1887. It was positioned near High Bridge at the entrance to the Dropping Well Estate, and until about 1947 was a scource of sulphur water, piped down from a spring at Bilton. It was later planted with flowers by the Dropping Well Estate, whose owner, on the sale of the estate, removed the public Jubilee Fountain to private land.

Below: The Knaresborough Carnival of 1938 followed the tradition set by the earlier Tradesmen's Processions. On this cart was a blacksmith plying his trade – Jack Danford, whose forge was in Fisher Street. Also on the cart is his daughter, Vera, who remembers her father making horseshoes as they rode along.

Lord Inman entering the Castle Yard on the 19 April, 1947, when he was given the Freedom of Knaresborough to celebrate his elevation to the peerage. He is accompanied by the Chairman of the K.U.D.C., Councillor J. Lingard, J.P. and Lady Inman can be seen between them.

Lord Inman of Knaresborough is welcomed by boys of nearby Castle School, shaking hands with Gordon Wright, whose father, the headmaster, is looking on with particular interest.

Lord Inman inspecting the guard of honour, which included these Air Cadets. This was a great occasion for Knaresborough. Philip Inman had risen from humble circumstances to become a peer of the realm. His positions included Chairman of Charing Cross Hospital and Chairman of the B.B.C., as well as Lord Privy Seal.

A representative gathering outside the Castle Girls School, including Scouts, Army and R.A.F. cadets, hears Lord Inman accepting the illuminated address from the town.

Lord Inman planting a tree to commemorate his visit to receive the Freedom of Knaresborough. On the right is Councillor Percy Broadbelt.

In 1951 Lord Inman presented the first civic chain of office to Councillor P. Broadbelt. The badge of office had been presented in 1930 by Col. W.F. Collins and Lady Evelyn Collins, but it had only been worn on a ribbon. This new chain consisted of 26 linked shields of silver gilt, each inscribed with the name of a Chairman of the Council – since 1974 the name of a Town Mayor.

Knaresborough House, seen from High Street, as it has looked since 1952, when various trees were felled. Built in 1768, probably to a design by John Carr, it has been the home of the Collins family, including our longest-serving vicar, the Revd Thomas Collins (incumbent from 1735 to 1788). It was bought by the K.U.D.C. in 1951, and here Knaresborough Town Council meets on alternate Mondays.

Knaresborough Urban District Council photographed on the occasion of the opening of Knaresborough House as the new Council offices. Front, from left: Councillors Jackson (E), Holch, Coles, Ackroyd (Chairman), Broadbelt, Cooper, Knutton. Back: Col. Wilkinson, Anderson (Surveyor), Brown (Town clerk) Councillors Kirk, Jackson (M), Emmett, the Sanitary Inspector and the Treasurer.

Part of the Georgian dining room of Knaresborough House, now used as the Council Chamber. Over the years the house has been put to many uses, including a period as a 'holiday home for poor families', opened by the Duke of Kent in 1936.

The first meeting of the Knaresborough Urban District Council in its new home of Knaresborough House in May 1951. Standing we see Councillor Percy Broadbelt, who had just been elected Chairman for the fourth time. He was a keen Labour supporter, for many years Secretary of the Working Men's Club. On the right is the Treasurer, Mr. C. Codd.

Left: The Water Carnival was revived after the Second World War, and amongst the people taking part in 1951 was Mrs. Amy Waite, here in the guise of Mother Shipton.

Below: The Water Carnival of 1953, the year of the Coronation of Elizabeth II, with a swan bearing the Queen, Zena Corps, who was 'Miss Knaresborough', and her retinue.

Following the Knaresborough Queen in the 1953 Water Carnival are the Scriven Queen, Jane Carey and the Rose Queen of Calcutt, Yvonne Youngson. In the background is a 26 foot model lighthouse with a revolving lantern.

Bathing beauties awaiting judgement at the 1953 Water Carnival. They are lined up by their entry numbers, but it so happens that the Leeds girl on the left was the winner. Was it this display of nubility which drew an estimated 7,000 spectators?

The Coronation of Queen Elizabeth II in June 1953 was celebrated not only by the Water Carnival but by all kinds of parties and outings. One of the most enterprising was organised by Frank Glover, who took a trip to Scarborough of people from the Meadowside area. Photographed here is just one of the happy groups which filled three big coaches.

History was made at an Annual Meeting of the Knaresborough Urban District Council held on the 27th May, 1957. The newly-elected chairman standing here was not a member of the Council, but Mr. George Hughes, who had just narrowly failed to be re-elected as a councillor.

Harry Corbett of 'Sooty and Sweep' fame firing the starting pistol in the first really successful Knaresborough Bed Race on 25 June, 1966. The previous year had been a kind of prototype, with only four teams, but from now on it went from strength to strength, with beds racing through the old streets and finally being floated across the river.

One of Knaresborough's most popular open-air events is the Boxing Day Tug of War, first held in 1968. Teams from the Half Moon and the Mother Shipton, on opposite sides of the river, pull across the water near Low Bridge. The very first Half Moon team, seen here, looks as though it knows about its future run of victories (23 wins, 3 losses and a draw). Front, from left: K. Hudson, T. Harper, Insp. R.W. McCollom, P. Hartley, J. Brooks, R. Park. Second from the right on the row behind is Bill Jones, the first captain.

The Town Twinning ceremony held on 5 June, 1970, sealed the partnership which had been formed between Knaresborough and the German town of Bebra the previous year. Here the Bürgermeister, August-Wilhelm Mende, is presenting to the Chairman, Councillor Neville Farmer, a model pair of wheels, symbolic of Bebra, a railway centre. Looking on is Friedrich Krönung, Chairman of the Bebra Council. This has proved to be a highly successful twinning with regular exchanges, not just by civic delegations, but at grass-roots level.

eight

Pupils and
Teachers

A feature of old Knaresborough from the eighteenth century onwards was a number of small private academies and dame schools. This is Miss Carrie Pullan's school in 1912. It was situated in Kirkgate, though this was taken in the garden of Richmond House, Waterside, the home of Marjorie Johnson, second from the left on the back row.

King James's Grammar school was founded in 1616 when the Revd Dr. Robert Chaloner of Goldsborough applied to King James I, who granted the school a charter bearing his portrait. It occupied a site overlooking the churchyard, where this later school building (1741) still stands.

A rare photo of Knaresborough Rural Secondary School in 1908. King James's had closed in 1905, but had now re-opened with Mr. G.W. Hefford as head, seen here with girl pupils as well as boys, the latter in early uniform of caps and collars.

Staff and pupils of King James's Grammar School, soon after the move to the York Road site in 1901. In the centre is the headmaster, Mr. H.J. Tyack Bake, who had been appointed in 1896 on a salary of £100 per annum. He earned it by modernising the curriculum, improving standards and ruling the boys with the strictest, hard-caning discipline.

The football team of the Old Boys of King James's Grammar School in the 1920/21 season. Front row, left to right: J. Brazier, H. Craven, H. Mainman, H. Taylor, G. Eddy. Second row: H. Bosworth, T. Oats, A. Robinson. Back: M. Fairman, H. Hudson, J. Wilson. The man in the hat on the left must be Councillor Henry Eddy, O.B.E., Chairman of the K.U.D.C. To the right are T. Vitty (in cap) and
R. Almond.

K.J.G.S First Eleven Football team, 1929/30. The Captain was W. Gregory, Vice-Captain R.J. Warren. Other players were J. Waddington, A.K. Tyfe, S.S. Uttley, D. Robinson, J. Lee, A. Linden, J.C. Pearce and E.W. Wood. On the left at the back is Mr. A.S.('Sam') Robinson, headmaster from 1922 to 1950. On the right is 'Taffy' Price, Welsh biology master and senior master, renowned disciplinarian and boxer of ears.

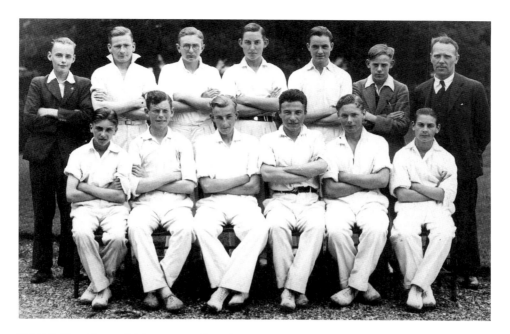

K.J.G.S. First Eleven Cricket team, 1936. The team is given as Buck, Varley, Hall, R. Linden, Robinson, Binks, Milner, Moore, Smith, Henry, B. Clayton, W. Linden. On the right is history master Mr. H.W. ('Strata') Street.

K.J.G.S. First Eleven football team, 1936/37. Mr. Street with Smith, Hall, Varley, Linden, Robinson, Wood. Front: Wilkinson, Keighley, B.Clayton, Henry (Captain) Garbutt, Kaye, Clayton. Results were 9 won, 1 lost (to Archbishop Holgate's, York) and 2 drawn.

Anyone for tennis? The 1938 team at K.J.G.S. Back row: P. Fairclough, J. Phillipson, M. Cooper, M. Pickles. Front: V. Marshall, K. Knowles, B. Trentholme.

'Jolly hockeysticks' smiles from this K.J.G.S. team of 1936/7. Front, left to right: W. Fryer, K. Herrington, M. Huddleston, B. Clayton, M. Cooper, B. Ghysels, P. Fairclough. (Back) Miss M. Craik, F. Fountain, M. Cassells, M. Pickles, V. Marshall, D. Baines, J. I'Anson. Miss Craik was house mistress of the Spartans. The other school houses were the Romans and the Trojans.

We can compare the photo above with another K.J.G.S. hockey team, thirty years on, in 1966. Front, left to right: J. Cosgrove, S. Todd, C. Beavis, W. Jackson, V. Todd. Back: -?-, K. O'Donnell, A. Palfreyman, H. Cheney, E. Scott, C. Medlycott. The houses now were Castle, Crag, Forest and Nidd.

The staff of Castle Boys School in 1934 with the headmaster who was appointed in 1934, Mr. Edward Wright, usually known as 'Gaffer' Wright, like his predecessor, 'Gaffer Smith'. To his right is Miss Jewitt, and to his left Mr. Percy Todd, deputy headmaster. The school in Castle Yard dates from 1814, when it was built as a Church of England National School. On comprehensive reorganisation in 1971 the Castle Schools moved down to the vacated premises of the County Secondary School.

Above: One of the classes – 47 children! – of Castle Girls School in 1920. Whereas the boys had their school in 1814 the girls were taught in the vicarage until their own school was built on the other side of Castle Yard in 1837. With their teacher, Miss Ella Land, are the following children, whose surnames were given to me by Winnie Patrick (now Mrs. Bentley) who had retained them in her memory 75 years later! Back row, left to right: Gregory, Burdett, Owram, Gray, Bowes, Kay, Thorp, Matthews, Robinson, Smith, Swales. Second row: Whitaker, Barnes, Atkinson, Grafton, Cliff, Cooper, Barwick, Allen, Barker, Brown, Broadbelt, Bell, Butterfield, Saunders, Thickett. Third Row: Ledgeway, Richardson, Watson, Bedford, Stephenson, Paxton, Wakefield, Pearson, Bramfitt, Hillyard, Brooks. Front row: Hall, Patrick, Clark, Pullan, Chapman, Headings, Whitley, Simpson, Wheelhouse. Mrs. Bentley is on the front row in the white pinafore. Behind her, wearing glasses, is Mary Cooper, later Mrs. Mary Mann, a much-respected local historian, who died in 1994.

Opposite above: The Castle Boys School football team in 1946, with the headmaster and his deputy, and the Castle ruins in the background. Back, left to right: D. Woolley, R. Farmer, G. Hodgson, C. Churchyard, C. Outhwaite, M. Waddington. Centre: P. Davey, G. Hill, W. Thompson (Captain), K. Fountain, B. Turner. Front: R. Frankland, G. Rolf.

Opposite below: Canon B.K. Kissack, Vicar of St. John's, being presented with a shooting-stick by the boys of Castle School on leaving Knaresborough in 1951. Canon Kissack, who had been in Knaresborough since 1935, like the incumbents before and after him, maintained the school's link with the Church of England which had founded it. Seen here with the Canon (from left) Mike Canterbury, Stuart Herrington, Ernest Clarkson (at back), Chris Atkinson (holding stick) and the headmaster, Mr. E. Wright.

A class in Castle Girls School in the 1950s – a school of traditional methods and discipline, and of happy memory to many Knaresborough girls.

A 1950s games period in the yard behind Castle Girls School, with skipping, ball-bouncing, hoops and vaulting poles.

The staff of Castle Girls School in 1956. Front, left to right: Miss E.A. Willis, Mrs. L. Borer, Mrs. D. Wignall (Headmistress), Miss D. Pratt, Mrs H.M. Saunders. Back: Student, Miss J. Bracken, Miss M. Barnes.

Four Castle Girls School winners of the annual prizes – the Stevens Bibles (in memory of Maria Stevens who died in 1810) and the Marshall Prize of clothing (following a bequest of Charles Marshall in 1823). A favourite photo of the author's, who later had the pleasure of teaching these girls French at King James's. From the left are Heather Brearley, Carol Milner, Ann Kaminski, Susan Welch.

The class of Miss Edith Willis at Castle Girls School in 1956. Back row, left to right: Jennifer Laird, Sandra Stocks, Marjorie Ryder, Susan Prest, Ann Whitaker, Sheila Corcoran, Susan Walker, Meryl Edwards, -?-, Janet Hamley, Beryl King. Middle: Marlene Parkyn, Jennifer Burrell, Edyth Bradley, Kathleen Learoyd, Margaret Owram, Jill Morgan, Janet Blackburn, Patricia Capin, Maureen Cleasby, Jean Lofthouse, Pat Cochrane. Front: -?-, Margaret Evison, -?-, Margaret Moore, Rhona Smith, Audrey Jones, Janette Watson, June Henderson, Elsie Burns, Susan Smith.

Opposite above: St. Mary's Roman Catholic school, dating from the building of the adjacent church in 1831, was teaching around 200 children by 1851. Here we see Miss Dyson, one of the teachers in the 1950s, with girls prepared for their First Communion. The school moved into modern premises in Tentergate Road in 1967.

Opposite below: Girls from Knaresborough Secondary Modern School in the days when Jack Thompson was headmaster. They kept as pets Larry the lamb and Wendy the goat. When Larry was eventually put into a field with other sheep he would always come to the girls when called.

The official opening of Manor Road Infants School took place on 21 November, 1949. This was the first purpose-built infants school in Knaresborough. The opening was performed by Mr. D. Hardman, M.P., Parliamentary Secretary to the Ministry of Education, who is seen here with children in their brand new classroom. On his right is Janet Malthouse, later a pupil, then a teacher, at King James's Grammar School. The little girl in front of Mr. Hardman is Sylvia Lumley.

Opposite above: A prize-giving at Knaresborough Secondary Modern school in the 1950s, showing Miss D.M. Hamilton (Senior Mistress), the Revd R.A. Talbot (Vicar of St. John's), Mr. L. Crosby (Headmaster) and Mr. Arthur Prest (Deputy Head) who served the school from 1925 to 1964.

Opposite below: The staff of Manor Road Infants School when it opened in 1949. Front row: Miss E. Makepeace (Mrs. D.W. Wilkinson), Miss I. Pinner (Headmistress), Miss M. Brown. Back row: Mrs. N. Metcalfe, Mrs. A. Burrell, Miss H. Gibbs, Miss M. Whitehead.

One of a regular succession of Nativity plays, this was staged at Manor Road Infants School in 1953, with the traditional cast of Mary, Joseph, Shepherds and Angels.

One of innumerable Christmas parties to round off the term, this one held at Manor Road Infants in 1960.

Mrs. Elizabeth Wilkinson's class at Manor Road Infants in 1966. When the school was opened in 1949 there were only four classrooms for 240 children. They soon took over the general-purpose rooms and reduced class sizes, but for many years there were rarely fewer than 40 children in a class.

King James's Grammar School in 1935. In the centre is the headmaster, Mr. A.S. Robinson. To the right of him is Miss E.H. Collins, Mr. J. Fairclough and Miss C.M. Andrew. To the left is Miss A. Wood, senior

mistress. Fifth to the left of the head is Miss D.M. Dews, and sixth is Mr. S. Norman, who retired in 1963 after 35 years at the school.

Music has long been an important tradition at King James's. In 1952 the conductor of the school orchestra, seen here in the gym which also served as a hall, was the headmaster, Mr. D.J. Stevens, who had succeeded Mr. A.S. Robinson in 1951.

Sixth Formers at work in the biology lab in 1952. Facilities in those days were comparatively restricted, but King James's Grammar School was renowned for high academic standards in both arts and science subjects.

Mr. Arthur Lancefield, when he was appointed headmaster of Knaresborough County Secondary School in 1959, taking over from Mr. L. Crosby. Known as 'Raggytash', he was in charge of around 400 children. When King James's comprehensive school was formed in 1971 he became the first deputy head.

The first group of candidates entered by Knaresborough County Secondary School for the new C.S.E. exam in 1966. In the centre is Mr. R.C. Simpson ('Sinbad'), maths teacher, appointed deputy head of the school in 1965. Front, from left: G. Wright, A. Dobson, N. Hampar, M. Zelch, G. Cotterill, M. Heath. Back: C. Malthouse, J. Metcalfe, S. Little, K. Batten, W. Riley, R. Hall.

Albert and Maud, the uncrowned king and queen of King James's Grammar School. Mr Albert Scurrah started as caretaker here in 1928, retiring in 1968. Mrs. Scurrah started even earlier, in 1925, retiring as cook-in-charge in 1965. This is how many former pupils will remember them. They were both lovable, hard-working characters, neither of whom would stand any nonsense.

The staff of King James's Grammar School in 1960. Front, left to right: Miss M. Durrans, Mrs. M. Winter, Mrs. M. Kettlewood, Mrs. M. Wilson, Miss B.M. Sawdon (Senior Mistress), Mr. F. Brewin (Headmaster), Mr. C.S. Walker (Senior Master), Mrs. E. Pinder, Mrs. E. Ellis, Mrs. N. Beaumont, Miss S. Russell. Centre: H. Horseman, ? Kerry, R. Beetham, Mrs M. Brown, Miss J. Botham, Miss M. Sewell, Mrs M. Rendle (Secretary), J.R. Metcalfe, A. Kellett, S. Norman. Back: W.J. Clark, W.H. Jowsey, R.F. Watts, M. Almond, T. Benstead, J.B. Jenkinson, P.R. Nudds, T.J. Sayles.

Opposite below: The first of several K.J.G.S. mock elections organised by the author, who ran the Debating Society, this one taking place in April, 1959. In front of this group of lively supporters are the candidates (from left) with their votes: T. Newell, Labour (68), D. Simmons, Liberal (52), T. Wood, Con. (200), D. Burn, Troglodyte (128), D. Poskett, Communist (33). Timothy Wood obviously gained from the experience, and went on to be elected a real-life Conservative M.P.

Overleaf: King James's Grammar School in 1971, the last year of its existence. By the time of its closure 'Knaresborough Grammar School' as it was often called, had given honourable service to the town and district for 353 years.

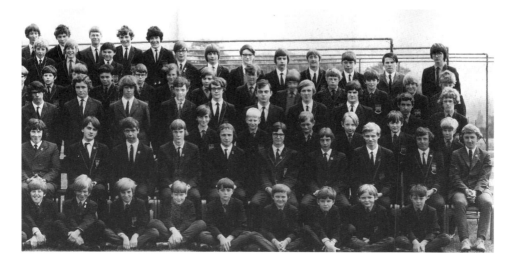

The last staff to serve at King James's Grammar School, June, 1971. Front, left to right: H. Horseman, T.J. Sayles, M. Winter, J.R. Metcalfe, B.M. Sawdon, F. Brewin, C.S. Walker, N. Beaumont, W.H. Jowsey, P.R. Nudds, A. Kellett. Centre: W. Sleight (Caretaker), J. Collins (Cook), M. Grint, V.A. Cohen (Secretary), –?–, J. Chatten, M. Sayles, T. Calvert, V. Barnwell, J. Coatman, –?–, P. Fulcher, F. Bailes. Back: M. Armsby, R.F. Watts, S.J. Herrington, M.A. Storr, J. Wilson, R.M. Hearld, P.E. Kearney, A.L. Kirkham, D.A. Briggs, M.A. Lowe, M.J. Wilkins. Frank Bailes served the school as groundsman for almost 33 years, retiring in 1974.

Opposite above left: We round off with the end of an era and the beginning of comprehensive education in the town. King James's School opened in September 1971, formed from the existing Grammar School and the County Secondary Schools of Knaresborough and Boroughbridge. The official opening (Tuesday, 29 February, 1972) was by Her Royal Highness, the Duchess of Kent, here seen receiving a bouquet. Behind is the headmaster, Mr. Frank Brewin.

Opposite above right: All smiles as the Duchess of Kent signs a special page in the visitors' book, with Councillor G.A. Holch, J.P., Chairman of the King James's Governors, looking on – and looking ahead.

Opposite below: Having put the clock back we must now move it forward again. An appropriate picture to end with, taken by one of Knaresborough's photographers from the past, Sid Horner.

Acknowledgements

Of the many people who have allowed me to borrow their photographs I would particularly like to thank Sir Arthur Collins, who kindly opened up treasured family albums, Mr. Chris Horner, who let me look through his late father's photographs, and Mrs. Isabel Garbutt, who gave me access to her meticulous collection of old postcards, as well as help with proof-reading. Others who have generously entrusted me with photographs or supplied especially useful information are as follows – with apologies to any I might have missed in the complex process of assembling a book from such diverse sources: D. Abbott, Ackrill Newspapers Ltd., P.D. Allott, Miss H. Alton, Mrs Moira Bailey, Miss E. Baines, Mrs. W. Bentley, H. Bingham, Mrs. E. Binks, Mrs Bradley, S. Brooks, F. Brown Ltd., Miss N. Buckle, Mrs S. Burchell, W.H. Campbell, Mrs. Jennifer Chatten, Mrs. J. Cheals, Mrs. M. Cooper, Mrs. W. Coupland, Mrs. E.M. Dinsdale, Mrs. J. Dunn, G.C. East, Mrs. M. Ellis, F. Newbould Photography Ltd., F. Glover, Mrs. M. Hall, D. Hallam, W.J. Hardacre, F. Healey, Mrs. R. Hill, Mrs. A. Holch, D. Horner, Mrs. P. Hunter, Mrs. A.P. Jervis, W.R. Jones, B. Jordan, N. Kent, Mrs. S. King, King James's School, Knaresborough Town Council, A. Lancefield, Mrs. E. Leahay, M. Linfoot, P. Longfellow, W.C. Malthouse, The Mary Mann Archive, D. Morris, T. Mudd, North Yorks. County Archives, North Yorks. County Library, K. Nowell, G. Outhwaite, E.W. Parsons, A. Prest, J.D. Prest, B. Reid (Knaresborough Fire Service), M. Robinson, J. Roper, E. Smith, Miss M.E. Stacey, Vollans Photography, G. Waite, Waterside Meat & Poultry, Mrs. C. Webb, L.J. Webster, Mrs. D.W. Wilkinson, Miss E.A. Willis, E. Wright.

Thanks, as always, to Pat for putting up with the chaotic accumulation of photos and notes, eventually reduced to order.